KITCHENS AND DINING ROOMS

KITCHENS AND DINING ROOMS

MARY GILLIATT

Photographs by

BRIAN MORRIS
and
Manfredi Bellati, Anthony Denney,
Roger Gain, Paul White

A Studio Book

THE VIKING PRESS · NEW YORK

For
my mother and
father who taught
me the full use of the
kitchen
and the dining room

Copyright © 1970 by Mary Gilliatt

Published in 1970 by The Viking Press, Inc.
625 Madison Avenue,
New York, 10022

Published in Canada by The Macmillan Company of Canada Limited

SBN 670-41413-1

Library of Congress catalog card number: 75-125245

Printed and bound in Great Britain

Acknowledgments for the decorative illustrations on these front pages appear on page 120

CONTENTS

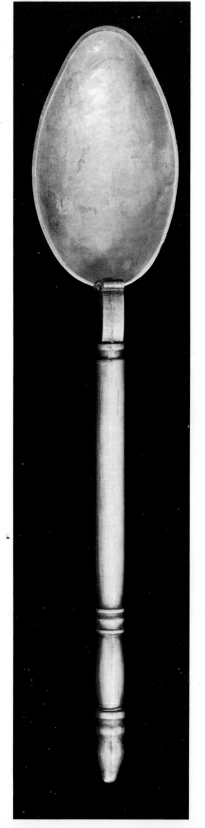

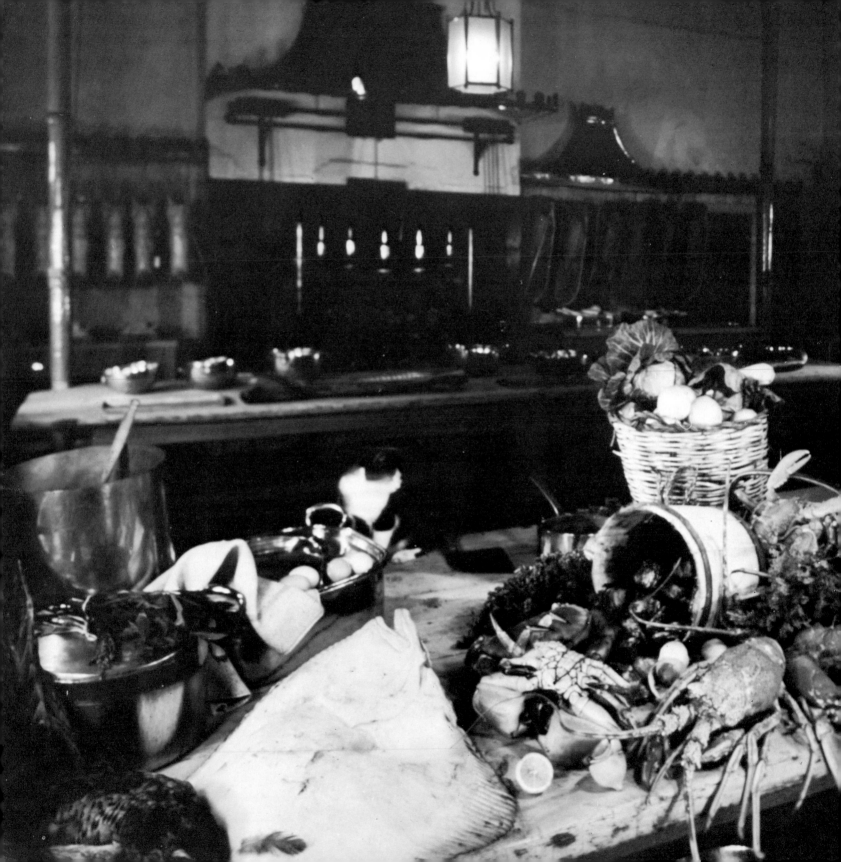

INTRODUCTION

A book about kitchens and kitchen decoration would be illogical if it failed to take into account the room or area where food was to be served. Not only is the one space the inevitable extension of the other, but as often as not these days, the kitchen and dining areas are in the same room anyway, just as they were in the distant past.

If the kitchen is the core of the house, the launching-pad, the basic machine for living with the primary function of preparing food, then the dining area – be it in the kitchen, hall, sitting room, or in a room of its own – should be as pleasurable a place as possible for consuming food.

Up until the end of the nineteenth century many well-to-do families, particularly in England and Europe, possessed kitchens which they hardly thought about, let alone visited, except perhaps for the occasional emergency, or for a tour of inspection. Kitchens were strictly for the servants. And in the great houses, they were often the middle area in that cycle of life described by Byron as, 'Born in the garret, in the kitchen bred. Promoted then to deck her mistress' head.'

Above all, the kitchen belonged to the cook, but its appointments were in direct proportion to the appetites and tastes of the head or heads of the household. The kitchen in the Royal Pavilion at Brighton, for instance (see opposite), indicates the gargantuan appetite of England's Prince Regent, and makes his notorious feasts and menus easier to understand. One imagines the kitchens of Surtees's lusty hunting heroes always aglow and alive with the sputtering and clanking of the spits with

Egyptian ladies at dinner
(Tomb of Rechmire in Thebes)

Opposite page: Kitchen in the Brighton Pavilion. (Photo: Anthony Denney/Condé Nast)

Above: Seventeenth-century kitchen scene. Engraving after Antonio Tempesta. *Left:* Nineteenth-century English knife. (Victoria and Albert Museum)

their trivets and skillets, the hiss of steam, though in fact they may well have been in possession of a belching, coal-consuming cast-iron 'kitchener' or range by then.

The 'middle classes' of Europe naturally followed the example of their so-called 'betters' as far as their purses allowed, allocating their kitchens to the furthest possible point from their living rooms. But for most families the kitchen was *the* room; in every sense the living room, just as it had been since the earliest times.

From farmhouse to cottage to early town-house, the kitchen was the place for almost every activity of domestic living. So much happened round the kitchen fire: bread-baking, roasting (for those who could afford, or manage to poach, the meat), preserving, medicine-making, sewing, spinning, love-making, quarrelling, births and deaths and the occasional bath.

From 1300 to 1860 kitchens changed very little. True, in the great mansions, the kitchen is known to have been brought in from the cold outhouse earlier than 1860,

Opposite: Italian nobleman at his table. Grimani Breviary. (Biblioteca Marciana, Venice)

but it remained as far distant as possible from the great hall, and subsequently from the dining room. In Regency days it became a little more convenient, but then regressed in Victorian times when the procurement of servants presented little problem.

For several hundred years the average equipment and furnishings for the kitchen in a well-appointed house consisted of at least three fireplaces: one for spits, one for boiling water and food, and the third for a primitive stone or brick oven for baking bread, which was first filled with blazing embers, and then, when thoroughly hot, emptied of ashes and filled with the dough. Pots and pans were suspended from racks, there was always a great trestle-table or two and later on there were dressers and perforated wooden cupboards called 'aumbries', for food, eating-utensils and linen. Floors were first plain, well-trodden earth and then stone-flagged, and sides of bacon, hams, dried fish, herbs, salt beef and strings of onions hung from the rafters, supplemented in America with strings of dried peppers and a store of apples and pumpkins.

In Tudor times the great spits were turned by boys, or by specially trained, short-legged dogs locked in cages set in the wall. The dogs were forced to pad interminably round and round to retain their balance. In the Carolean period, the larger houses benefited from a very early and sadly inconvenient form of kitchen-range with a confined fire and adjacent ovens. These ranges were introduced into America early in the eighteenth century.

Pennsylvania was the first American State to introduce metal and hot-air drums and these were considered a great improvement over the fire and spit. Soon china stoves were being advertised, and in 1742 Benjamin Franklin designed a very practical stove which burned coal and wood. The stove was made free-standing because, as Franklin remarked, with a fireplace, 'a man is scorched before, while he is frozen behind'.

The Franklin stove did service, with many variations, until the middle of the nineteenth century, not that it is not still a treasured antique. But, in the 1860s, the flat-topped, cast-iron kitchen-range appeared, and was soon in more general use. Kettles and pots came off their hooks, the heavy iron containers began to be replaced by lighter ware of coated steel, and with the beginning of piped water, the housewife had at least a little store of hot water with which to wash dishes.

The first gas cooker was shown at the Great Exhibition in London in 1851, but did not really come into its own in America until the 1880s. The real revolution in the kitchen started after the first clumsy, almost unrecognizable electric cooker was placed on exhibit at the Chicago Columbia Exhibition of 1893.

Opposite: Kitchen in the Saugus Iron Works House, Massachusetts.
(Photo: Samuel Chamberlain)

Tulipware pottery dish.
(Pennsylvania Museum of Art)

10

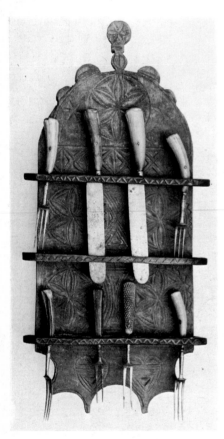

Early American rack with knives and forks. (Metropolitan Museum of Art)

Since the First World War each successive decade has swelled the advance of the servant to the factory and the equivalent retreat of the mistress to the kitchen. Radical changes in the design of kitchens and equipment (and menus) came about, led strongly by the matriarchal society of America. In fifty years wooden sinks were replaced by sinks made of iron, zinc, copper, porcelain and finally of steel. The vacuum cleaner took over from the ubiquitous broom, the ice-house in the garden gave way to the icebox and subsequently to the electric refrigerator and the deep freeze, and the laundry tub, washboard and wringer were transformed into the washing machine and spin-drier. By 1930 there were nineteen types of electrical appliances on the U.S. market; today there are around one hundred.

By the end of the Second World War, designers had turned kitchens into smallish streamlined boxes. Probably it was resentment at being tied to the stove after their freedom during the war that led Anglo-American females (their European counterparts have never really doubted their role) to the aseptic, clinical, easily wipeable finishes, the trim, hygienic white boxes to house the trim, hygienic packaged foods. Certainly, it looked as if all traces of the cluttered, lived-in rustic kitchen had gone forever. The appliance manufacturers, the frozen food kings, the canners and the food merchants exploited to the hilt the female desire to get out of the kitchen just as quickly as she could.

Having reached the stage where the kitchen seemed more to resemble an operating-theatre than a comfortable place in which to cook, with food carefully concealed behind prim doors and cooking smells minimized by air-extractors, we arrived at the ridiculous situation of importing such decorative touches as strings of plastic onions and garlic, plastic curtains and tablecloths embellished with fruits and vegetables and plastic surfaces emulating wood – all with the false idea of bringing back a 'homey' look into the kitchen.

Happily, in recent years, the situation has adjusted itself on many fronts. Perhaps this is because woman cannot be kept away from her natural instincts for very long? At any rate, more general prosperity, increasing travel, an unending deluge of new ideas from women's columns and glossy magazines, and, more particularly, the ballooning popularity of books on cooking that stimulate interest in cuisine, have all conspired to restore domesticity and warmth to the kitchen. Capsule kitchens – one-unit kitchens with every appliance attached to a central island or robot – have exploded on the scene from time to time like over-heated chestnuts, but for the moment they have had little impact.

Eighteenth-century pine kitchen.
(The Henry Francis du Pont Winterthur Museum)

Glass rolling-pin.

Larding-needles and case.

Currently, kitchens appear to have the best of both worlds: the efficiency of modern appliances and the warmth of natural textures like wood and brick and ceramic tile. The appearance on the market of *batteries de cuisine* from Spain, Portugal, France and Scandinavia – countries where the traditions never really died – have all added to their quality. Just because help is so hard to come by, the kitchen has once again become a personal room and at the same time a more sophisticated one.

The advantages of having the space for a family room, a living room-kitchen, are manifold, even if there is a dining room as well. Old houses that people refused to buy in the 1940s and 1950s because of the rambling size of their kitchen quarters are now being eagerly sought for that very reason. Similarly, old kitchen utensils are being ardently tracked down for use as well as for decoration.

Just as America led the way into the revolution of convenience and hygiene in the kitchen, so it has led the way with what might be termed the romantic – but practical – revival. Even the most determined modernist now has an honesty about his approach to kitchen design, a lustiness, which is heartening.

Dining rooms have seldom been very personal rooms; distinguished, grand, comfortable, opulent they may have been, but rarely with that idiosyncrasy often possessed by bedrooms, living rooms or bathrooms. In castle, manor-house and farm, from Saxon days up until the fourteenth century, people ate solidly sitting on benches at long trestle-tables in the hall. After the meal, the trestles were stacked away, and at night family and retainers lay down among the layers of mouldering rushes strewn with bones and refuse to sleep *en communauté*. By the fourteenth century, the solar or withdrawing room was occasionally used as a more intimate dining room when the family wanted a little privacy. Nevertheless, the hall was still used for all formal occasions, and the contrast of rich costume and rush floor, gold and silver plate, flickering rush-lights, smoking fires and flaring torches is a pretty thought. Decoration would have been superfluous. More usually though, food was served on plain wooden dishes which were shared by two or three people; or more commonly still it was served on a trencher – which was a large wooden platter – or a large slice of coarse bread.

In the fifteenth century, a parlour was added to the solar and used for dining. It was typically wood-panelled with a stone fireplace and lit by rush-lights and candles. But it was not until the end of the sixteenth century that small dining rooms began to appear for that purpose alone, decorated in bright colours with arms and armour, stags' heads and flowers. There were still very few chairs in use; those that existed were reserved for the head of the family (the origin of chairman) and everyone else sat on stools or benches.

During the first half of the seventeenth century, real dining rooms were built into most houses of any size and were furnished with a settle, stools, a large table, smaller side-tables, a cupboard, buffet and an upholstered chair or two. Wainscoting became more and more the general medium for wall covering; it was often ornately carved, and the designs, contrary to our general notions today, were picked out in colour. Framed paintings, particularly portraits in oils, became more common, and sculpture, carvings and pottery began to be used decoratively in the more important rooms.

By this time the rushed and stone-flagged floors had given way to polished floor boards, though rugs were rare and expensive. In Jacobean times, the huge refectory tables started to shrink a little and often they were replaced by the draw-table which had a sliding top that could be pulled out to accommodate extra people. The chief innovation, however, was the gate-legged table, although it was not fully developed until after 1650.

Curiously, it was not until the early eighteenth century that chairs came into general use. Then a dining room in a prosperous household might consist of a gate-legged table, a screen, bureau cabinet, a wine-cooler, and a long-case clock, as well as chairs. There would be a plastered ceiling, panelled walls with bolection mouldings and doors and window-frames with matching mouldings. The floor would be polished, with a carpet in a brightly coloured wool, and there might be a carved and painted wood chandelier and silver sconces.

By the middle of the eighteenth century, walls might be panelled in pinewood and stained or painted an olive-green. Mouldings were often carved and gilded, the fireplace might have a marble surround and a steel fire-basket. There would still be a bureau cabinet, perhaps made of walnut, and very likely a pair of Chinese porcelain vases. The table too might be of walnut. In America, formal dining rooms were generally based on English or French styles; but usually the rooms were less ornate and possessed a lighter, simpler kind of elegance than their European counterparts.

At the end of this glorious eighteenth century, there would be plaster ceilings and friezes, Classical decoration in very low relief, plaster, sometimes with a painted decoration on the walls, a carpet to fit into the scheme with the ceiling design, sash-windows with silk curtains on wood curtain poles. Glass chandeliers, candel-

Measure.

Lemon-squeezer of yew and silver.

abras in alcoves, a mahogany dining table and chairs decorated with marquetry and brass stringing would complete the main furnishings. And in a bay-window would stand a circular inlaid breakfast table.

I mention these items in some detail for whenever one thinks of the classic or traditional dining room, it is almost inevitably a re-creation of this sort of decoration . . . or of the Regency period that followed with its rosewood chiffoniers, mirror-backed shelves, eagle-surmounted mirrors, striped silk curtains and chair seats, and wool carpet.

By this time the side-table had given way completely to the sideboard, and by Queen Victoria's prime all the lightness and grace of the eighteenth and early nineteenth centuries had given way to dirty ochre-coloured lincrusta ceilings, deep-patterned paper friezes, red-patterned flocked wallpaper and dark brown varnished lincrusta paper for the dado. Paintwork was dark brown and varnished and strongly patterned rugs or carpets covered the floor.

The turn of the century was the heyday of reproduction furniture which people seemed to trust more than they trusted wormy old originals. Sheraton, Chippendale, Adam and Jacobean styles were all copied; but although rooms got a little less heavy it seemed incumbent on our immediate forbears to eat in an atmosphere of deepest gloom, a state that they clearly felt was warm and domesticated. In the jumpy 1920s and 1930s we went to the opposite extreme and dined in a lightness and brightness, a sharpness of focus that was far from the subtlety and warmth of previous decades.

Now with the problems of space engendered by increasing population, it is common for a whole apartment to be made out of a nineteenth-century *salon*. And we dine in the kitchen or the hall or the sitting room, and more rarely in a special room originally designed for the purpose.

It is still hard, though, to find a really idiosyncratic dining place. On the whole, dining rooms fall into the familiar historical categories, with the difference that now people search for, and highly prize, the original furniture. And perhaps that is sensible. The serious diner does not want his attention distracted and the unserious diner does not mind where he eats at all.

I would emphasize that the main point of the book is to give examples of the current trends in the decoration of kitchens and dining rooms without losing sight of their historical context. It is meant, above all, to give ideas.

For the sake of convenience, the examples are broken down into a series of

Photograph by Bill Brandt.

Opposite: Desserte. Henri Matisse.
(Edward G. Robinson Collection)

categories. Cooks – that is to say, the great cooks and great cookery writers in the public eye – are given their own section which is placed before anything else. This is only logical, because one supposes that they should act as an example to us all. This is followed by sections on serious kitchens, belonging to people who, although not professional cooks, take their cooking very seriously; country – or country-type – kitchens which are really just a contemporary extension of the classic kitchen format; sophisticated kitchens – a departure from the normal formula, which, as I have been at pains to show, entails more than just gilding the kitchen stove; and purist, or unadulterated and uncompromising, kitchens where function dominates, but by no means obscures, form.

After these, again I think logically, follow kitchen-dining rooms, the natural successors to the living room-kitchens of earlier times. In a section on traditional dining rooms, I have tried to choose a number of rooms whose owners have employed an intelligent, rather than a slavish, interpretation of the past. Modern dining rooms – in this context, original dining rooms – were difficult to find, but all the more worth photographing. And I have ended with a series of dual- and sometimes treble-purpose dining rooms – rooms which have been dictated by lack of space and are all the more decorative and ingenious for that lack.

As I have said, this is a book on decoration. There is no use resisting the fact that it is important – at least for the spirit – to prepare and eat food in a well-designed and congenial atmosphere. This does not mean that one should possess the best and latest in kitchen equipment, simply that one should make as sympathetic an environment as possible for the equipment one has.

Taste and determination, a sense of order and comfort, *are* more important than money. I would like to think that this book will encourage many people to make their cooking more of a pleasure and less of a drudgery.

Fruits and vegetables heaped in a kitchen designed by photographer Anthony Denney.

COOKS' KITCHENS

Since the kitchen is, after all, for cooking, it is clear that the professional cooks and gourmets – in this case the men and women who also write and talk about that subject for a living – should set an example in their kitchen arrangements for all to follow. The pictures on these pages show how all extraneous ornament is eschewed. Pots, pans, the general *batterie de cuisine*, give enough variety, enough pattern and warmth to make these kitchens wholly appetizing rooms. Pine dressers, *armoires* and old buffets are stuffed with kitchen clutter; peg boards are strung with pans and instruments to make simple 'still-life' compositions; and tables and chairs are tough. It is also interesting to note that the cooking equipment is not particularly technical or advanced. There is little evidence of those rows of buttons and switches that have made some modern kitchens seem more like the instrument panel in a jet plane.

Above: A Victorian spice-box in the author's possession. Shaped like an old brown tin trunk, it has six compartments, and a small nutmeg-grater attached to the inside of the lid.

Opposite page: Philip Brown, who lives in California, is a subtle, delicate cook with a well-used clutter of tools. In this kitchen in Pasadena an uncounted number of copper and metal pans swing from a semicircular steel rack launched above a central island chopping-board. A magnetic knife-rack runs the length of one of the windows like a frieze. The supporting posts at the side of the chopping-block are slung with every sort of utensil and kitchen aid. Underneath, the canisters are decorated with Toulouse-Lautrec posters.

Left and opposite : Mrs Elizabeth David has probably done more to revive the British interest in cooking than anyone else. The gentle, lyrical, appetizing prose in her various books make them pleasant bedside reading as well as practical guides. Her famous kitchen shop in London sells humble country ware, the best Provençal pots, the sharpest knives, the ripest olive oil. In a sense she has managed to distil the essence of French and Italian cooking as no one has before her. Her kitchen is full of well-tried, well-loved, well-used objects, stored in a series of buffets, *armoires* and dressers with everything easily to hand.

Mrs Julia Child, the grand lady of American TV cookery, has a neat, light, lime-green and white kitchen in Boston. It is crammed with copper pans and burnished steel and earthenware jars full of spoons and knives. A detail of one of her peg boards hooked with a gentle series of saucepans, frying-pans and skillets shows how effective these simple arrangements can be.

Opposite: Craig Claiborne of *The New York Times* has a kitchen in his Long Island home which bears out the thesis that kitchens – except for a few lapses and capers in taste and improvement in equipment – have hardly changed since Tudor times. Brick walls and floors, thick wood working-tops, cooking paraphernalia slung from the ceiling and walls . . . the recipe is much the same.

James Beard is another of the great cooks. His New York kitchen seems all soft greens and russets interspersed here and there with tomato-red. Etched pineapples decorate the end wall, copper pans and spice-racks the other. His U-shaped working counter is inset with chopping-boards, hot-plates and cooking-rings. A huge marble top holds a clutter of knives and funnels and skillets, and great earthenware pots stand round the floor.

Robert Carrier, an American living in London, has had enormous success with his books, his cookery cards, his shops within shops, and his Islington restaurant. He likes to talk almost as much as he likes to cook and eat, so his kitchen with its vine-strung patio is geared for entertainment. With its scalloped copper canopy, blue and yellow ceramic tiles on wall and floor, plants, and green, brown and white checked seat covers, it is rather more decorated, rather less deliberately utilitarian than the other cooks' kitchens.

SERIOUS
KITCHENS

Serious kitchens – or at least kitchens belonging to people who *seriously* like cooking – share the common denominator of being well stocked, well planned and having a particular atmosphere which is not just a compendium in the air of years of crushed garlic and stock-making and the slow cooking of ragouts, but a warmth and sense of ease which appears to be an appendage of the gentle art of cooking. Whether they are large or small, crammed into corridors or perimeters of rooms, these kitchens are obviously used and enjoyed by their owners.

Lorna Dawson has an extremely efficient galley kitchen in her apartment in Cambridge, Massachusetts. The open wood shelves massed with jars and glasses, white china and brown earthenware; the white-boarded ceiling and wood working-top surrounded by racks of knives and spice-jars make a virtue out of convenience.

Opposite: Howard Perry Rothberg II has a splendid collection of pottery chickens, shelves and shelves full, in his pleasant wood and brick kitchen in New York.

31

Jon Bannenburg, the English designer, is a good cook himself, and he has created this eminently workable kitchen for Mr and Mrs Morgan's beautiful Georgian house in Essex. He dislikes cupboards above counter-tops (which has been the usual format for some years now) and has built here an L-shaped unit round a wall oven which he has inset with cooking-rings, working surface, chopping-board, sink and dish-washer. Cup-boards are full length with herring-boned wood doors. A slatted rack is suspended from the ceiling – just as it was in medieval days – for pots and casseroles.

Left and opposite : Another black and white kitchen, this time in New York, proves that black, though not an obvious choice, is unusually successful in the pinpointing of culinary colour. Even the appliances are painted black. The light fixture, a ring of bare bulbs, is a dominant feature; so is the library of books on cooking, not to mention the random design of the utensils hung on the peg board.

Above and opposite : This London kitchen designed for Mr and Mrs Cob Stenham by architect Michael Brown is tough, uncompromising, well planned, almost New Brutalist. It was carved out of the original sitting room in a Victorian house. Mr Brown retained the old pine fireplace, bricked the floor, painted the walls a muted green and covered the ceiling with pine boards. Also, he designed a series of chunky full-length and counter-height cupboards with other cupboards above. The rest of the decoration lies in the unexpected ram's head over the fireplace and its row of Mexican plates, the wood carving on one wall, and the odd pots and dishes.

Above and opposite: Terence O'Flaherty, the *San Francisco Chronicle*'s columnist, has managed to cram a remarkable amount into a smallish space. Not only has he crammed, he has patterned his cramming with enormous skill. Interesting spoons are slung across one window like stalactites, and spices clutter the brick edge that runs round the room with built-in stove and storage space for saucepans. The cane bull's head, half-framed as it were in garlic bulbs, is set on a brilliant yellow wall, and an ancient curved and complicated iron rack, set above a huge old red-japanned coffee-tin to run almost the length of the brick working surface, is stacked with casseroles, fish-kettles, teapots, jars and white china ornaments.

Opposite: Jars, bottles, pots and utensils are arranged with loving care in a cosy room that seems to be all brown and red and white. The barley-twist columns on the mirror (which gives the illusion of a room twice the size), the slender steel rack above the island sink with its sturdy wood working-top and inset appliances, the capacious wood dresser . . . and the cat . . . all contribute to the unique appearance of Mr and Mrs Pat Owen Martin's California kitchen.

Left and above: Laurie Stanley Moore, who teaches at New York's Pratt Institute, not only uses the more conventional piles of plates and dishes as decoration on their own, but also masses packaged goods and cans on open shelves instead of tucking them away behind cupboard doors. The resulting colour scheme, together with the slash of red in an alcove containing telephone and clock, is rich and warm. Incidentally, the kitchen is sited on a balcony which overlooks the children's playroom and is thus doubly practical.

COUNTRY
KITCHENS

In this urban age of ribbon development, burgeoning new towns and mushrooming housing, the rustic has become precious, rare – a quality to be treasured, preserved, emulated. The kitchen was always preeminently rustic up until the middle of the last century and perhaps one might even say up until the recent age of plastics and frozen food. And today it is interesting to note how many designers are turning to the past for inspiration while retaining, of course, the most advanced kitchen equipment.

The Scandinavians have hardly swerved from their traditional devotion to wood; and one would expect the Spanish, the Swiss, the Japanese and the English, in the country at least, to be equally loyal. What is surprising is the extent to which the urbanites of New York, Paris and London have forgone the practicality of laminated plastic and the gleam of convenient metal to emulate the sophisticated country-kitchen look. This trend is typified by some of the following examples.

In this Japanese farmhouse the kitchen is truly simple. A semicircle of stone provides space for cooking and washing the dishes. A kettle sits on a minuscule stove, and the collection of buckets and other containers are ready for the preparation of that most delicate and esoteric of cuisines.

Opposite page: Two American painters, Don Kunkle and Carl Van der Volt, built a house on the Spanish island of Ibiza much as the country people of South America would have built their homes. In the kitchen they incorporate an ancient stove in a cement block to provide cooking facilities (they only burn wood) and built stout wooden shelving to hold earthenware dishes and cast-iron pots. The walls are of plain white plaster, and the floor is brick.

43

Below: A kitchen in an old mill-house. The sturdy wood and white-painted brick are perfectly in keeping with the building which belongs to Sir Lesley and Lady Martin, near Cambridge, England.

Above and opposite: Christo Coetzee, the painter, lives in a part fifteenth-century, part nineteenth-century house built in the rock face near Alicante, Spain. His kitchen is simple, on different levels, wandering down corridors, up steps and ledges just as the rest of the house does. A simple blue-tiled floor, some blue-painted furniture, a touch of blue in the ceramics and paintings . . . and the rest consists of basketwork, a wooden hay-rake, an ancient sink, a tiny stove.

This kitchen in a house near Helsinki uses mostly old wood and old equipment. At mealtimes the stove unit is closed off as shown above. Walls are white, and a black and white Marimekko cloth is on the table. The house belongs to Rita Salo, who works for Marimekko in Finland, painting wood jewellery.

Lord and Lady Rendlesham's farmhouse kitchen has stone floors, nut-brown-painted plaster walls, and a long wooden refectory table with benches. The old kitchen-range (supplemented by more modern appliances) is built into the sink unit and working-counter. The only other remnant from the twentieth century is the red Magistretti chair.

Opposite: Another ancient kitchen, this time in Jutland, and belonging to E. Moltke Nielsen. Semicircular windows are carved out of the thick walls. A long counter-shelf is suspended from the ceiling and one of the walls. The stove, refrigerator, sink and cupboards are unobtrusively fitted into a working-counter below the windows, while another row of cupboards has been carpentered above.

Opposite: Peter Knapp, an art director, made this kitchen in his Paris apartment in the Passage Choiseuil. He burnt the pine-boarded walls with a flame-gun to give them an authentic Swiss country look, and then contrasted them with shiny white doors.

Above right: Wood is used heavily in this Oslo kitchen. The stove controls are inset between wooden drawers, and both hob and sink are let into a chunky teak counter-top. Old wood shelves are suspended on the wall.

Right: Another Norwegian wooden kitchen. This time the structure is entirely of wood with a well-designed complex of sturdy wood shelves, drawers, cupboards and counter-tops. Shelves are set across the window in a grid pattern, and the browns and terracottas of the casseroles look well against the predominant gold of the pine cladding.

Golden wood and brick are featured in this Norwegian kitchen, which is solid, chunky, unassuming and warm against the snow outside.

Opposite: The costume designer, Edith Head, owns an authentic early Mexican adobe in California. The kitchen has a terracotta tiled floor and tiled working-tops. Mexican earthenware pots are arranged with attractive symmetry on and around wooden shelves in the centre of the room. Mexican iron filigree-work hangs on one wall and the ceiling-boards are washed with white.

Left: A lovely and comforting kitchen featuring whitened brick and plaster and an antique cast-iron stove. Gingerbread moulds hang from a long strip of wood by the door, a string of garlic hangs from the skylight, and an early American rocking-chair sits in front of a butcher's chopping-block. For the rest the sculptor Tino Nivola, who lives in Long Island, has assembled a variety of trays, wicker baskets, stone jars and pots, cast-iron pans and casseroles.

Opposite: A tiled floor, pink and white gingham café curtains, a brass rack suspended between the wood shutters for slinging baskets, bright pots and pans, a wood ceiling and walls with unobtrusive modern appliances, make this London kitchen a splendid marriage of rusticity and convenience. Elizabeth Meacock designed it for the Rt Hon Anthony and Mrs Nutting.

SOPHISTI-CATED KITCHENS

Above and opposite page: This blue and white tiled kitchen belongs to Kenneth J. Lane in New York. He has used a number of different designs and shapes of tile with great skill. In addition, the brickwork, wood units and the good-looking pans and saucepans all contribute to the room's unique character.

The sophisticated kitchen – as we would use the term nowadays – is not the despoiled naturalness that most dictionary definitions would have us believe. It is strange how we have managed to change a pejorative term into an admiring one through regular misuse. Today, we would think of sophisticated kitchens as rooms that make decisive use of opulent materials, that take the simple and work it into something striking; rooms that are sometimes as much living rooms as kitchens in so far as the apparatus of cooking is not the first thing that strikes the eye. Or we think of rooms that cleverly play around with shapes and colour. But if the sophisticated kitchen is more striking or good-looking than it is workmanlike in appearance, this does not mean that the work done in it is any the less good.

Charles Moore, Professor of Architecture at Yale, tore out most of the inside of his old house in New Haven, Connecticut, and rebuilt it in a completely idiosyncratic way. His kitchen makes great use of cut-out shapes and discs, the bright Pop colours focusing well with the pair of plaster columns.

Brown-grey and dark blue tiles are used in a subtle geometric pattern in Veira da Silva's beamed kitchen in Paris. The stove, double sink and refrigerator are embedded into the stainless-steel-topped unit with more wood units above.

Left: The stainless-steel tiled and travertine island in the middle of Jon Bannenburg's London kitchen incorporates sink, waste-disposer, working-top, cooking-rings and hot-plate. Full-length cupboards round the room hold everything from refrigerator to stove to food and utensil storage. Red-lacquered beams divide the room sectionally. The screens are made from slotted wood. At the far end of the room, under the window, is a scrubbed table with Provençal chairs.

Right: A large country kitchen designed by David Hicks. Walls are covered in ceramic tiles, the floor is quarry tiled, and sinks and cooking-rings are sunk at intervals into the U-shaped working surface. A useful stainless-steel rack runs the whole length of these working surfaces.

Stainless-steel tiles, stormy grey walls, and a great long refectory table and bench add distinction to Lord and Lady Rendlesham's London kitchen. A dresser holds pewter plates, an early pair of scales, more stainless steel, dark brown earthenware and white pottery.

Delicate blue and white ceramic tiles are used with originality at the top of the extractor hood and round the cornice of this kitchen. Tiles also outline the window and come to waist-level in the dining area beyond the doorway. The floor is also tiled – in terracotta. A chopping-board at the end of the hob area, blue and white canisters and blue and white casseroles complete this beautifully integrated room belonging to Mr and Mrs Leslie Land on Long Island.

Opposite: Ceramic tiles with animal, vegetable and fruit motifs decorate the walls and table in Mr and Mrs Wurzberger's Baltimore kitchen. Cupboards, ceiling and door are painted a subtle greeny beige, and the panelling is outlined in a darker grey-green. A prize collection of books on cooking is recessed into the far wall and a candelabra hangs attractively over the table. The designer is Ed Benesch.

PURIST
KITCHENS

Above and opposite page: White walls, smooth wood surfaces and a terracotta tiled floor add to the good looks of this kitchen with its crisp clear lines and soaring heights. Cupboard knobs look like the headed pins used as markers on a wall map or chart. Hugh Newell Jacobsen designed the house for a Washington client, then eventually bought it for himself.

Purist kitchens pay no homage to rusticity or prettiness. Uncompromisingly they use twentieth-century units and ingredients. They are inevitably spare of line, extremely well planned and easy to work in. This does not preclude colour, but they are often pure white and beautifully detailed. Most purist kitchens are designed by architects – usually for themselves.

Above and opposite: The kitchen in the house architect Tom McNulty designed for his family in Lincoln, Massachusetts, is set in a pure curve of concrete within a house that is full of curving vistas; a house that is like a great piece of sculpture set in downy wild-flowered fields at the side of a lake. The symmetry of the golden wood, white top and bands of drawer fronts stretch in beautiful perspective.

Left: Architects Joan and Chester Sprague have used a colour scheme of dark purple-blue and white with touches of red in this kitchen, which is part of the conversion job they did on their old house in Cambridge, Massachusetts. Ceiling planes add interest, and long shelves full of glasses, spice-jars and white china are contrasted with chunky earthenware pots and an interesting collection of old green bottles.

Opposite: Some of the wall and half of the cupboard units in this kitchen are in rich, dark cherrywood; the other units are steel-grey and white-topped. Yellow pottery cups and saucers add a dash of brilliant colour. The interesting ribbed ceiling is constructed of concrete. The kitchen, belonging to architect Arthur Elrod, is in the house he designed at Palm Springs, California.

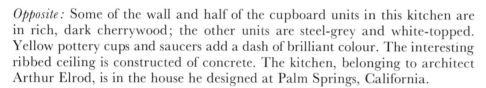

Left: White units are contrasted with patterned tiles in green and brown in this large kitchen designed by Elizabeth Meacock for Mr and Mrs Samuelson in London. The copper-rimmed lights and copper saucepans match the copper extractor hood over the stove.

An attractive combination of a blue and yellow tiled floor, natural wood walls and ceiling, decorative panels, and an antique stove make up Mr and Mrs Franc Shor's kitchen-dining room in their Washington house.

Opposite : White Saarinen table and chairs grace this modern, all wood Washington kitchen belonging to Mrs Mary Swift. The upper cupboard, hung with a bright poster, appears to float over the lower counter area.

KITCHEN-DINING ROOMS

The kitchen-dining room has become such a convenient part of people's lives these days that it has almost ousted the traditional dining room. And certainly the idea is a most practical one for week-end and holiday houses. Some of the rooms in this section might easily have been grouped with the country kitchens or serious kitchens, but because they are either the sole eating area in a house or are used more often than the normal dining room, they have been included here.

The kitchen-dining room – as opposed to the kitchen-living room – is, of course, very much a twentieth-century innovation. But as almost everyone now is his own cook, at least to some extent, this kind of room is the logical answer for unbroken conversations, last-minute dishes, hot food and the minimum of fuss and bother. It should be comfortable, relaxing, easy, natural. A place in which one *could* spend the whole evening.

Opposite and above: White walls and ceilings, highly polished floors and an island block inset with a beautiful blue and white Mexican basin make Mr and Mrs Hogle's San Francisco kitchen-dining room a bright and cheerful place to visit. In addition, the large windows take full advantage of the magnificent view over the wooded mountainside.

Opposite: A brick floor, scarlet-stained rafters, an old Victorian pine dresser standing against the wall which divides the eating from the cooking area, an antique oil-lamp and brilliantly coloured fibreboard table and chairs make up this kitchen-dining room designed by Paul William White for the author. The cotton blinds are in a pattern of brown and red on white.

Right: The bentwood chairs and bead curtains add character to the dining area of this kitchen-dining room owned by the Finnish sculptor, Erkke Haïvoja. Grass paper is pasted between the ceiling joists in a Japanese-Finnish cohesion. The floor is brick.

A wood ceiling and a tiled floor help preserve the simplicity of this English kitchen-dining room belonging to Mr and Mrs Terence Conran in Suffolk. Cupboard units, sink, refrigerator and stove are all located down one wall, and bentwood chairs surround the pine table. The blind is a green-blue William Morris cotton.

Opposite: The tiled kitchen area of this panelled kitchen-dining room is divided by a counter with louvred cupboards. Rush-seated chairs surround a mahogany table. The owner is Jacques Charron of the *Comédie Française*.

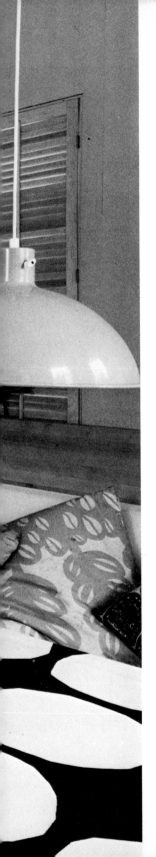

Three views of the kitchen-dining room in architect Ben Thompson's house in Cambridge, Massachusetts. The main ingredients are brick floors, wood units, a pair of butcher's chopping-blocks and a stove set in a brick plinth which divides the eating and working areas. The tablecloth (in the view on the opposite page) is by Marimekko.

Above and opposite: An old house was converted by ripping out half of one of the floors so that an attractive balcony sitting room could be created. The wall support of the sitting room, painted a brilliant chrome-yellow, divides the kitchen from the dining area. Walls are stripped to bare brick on two sides of the room and the round wood table has olive-green polypropylene chairs. Blinds are an orange and scarlet Marimekko fabric. Architect Ben Moore redesigned this house in Boston.

Left and below: Most of the ground floor of a Late Victorian house in London was converted into a kitchen-dining room. Designer Paul Anstee used beams and employed a series of old buffets for storage space, even taking some to pieces to furnish further cupboard doors. He also installed a black and white marble floor and brought in the French chairs and table to achieve the atmosphere of a Provençal kitchen.

Above and left: A warm coffee and cream coloured floor, dark brown wood units and shelving which displays a collection of blue and white china, are featured in this kitchen-dining room belonging to columnist Maxine Cheshire in Washington.

This room in Ralph Ducasse's old San Francisco house looks splendid with its dresser and refectory table, white china, Oriental carpet and collection of animal prints. The kitchen working area is round the corner.

Right : The brilliant blue walls of the dining-kitchen area in Charles Moore's house at Sea Ranch, California are contrasted with the square design painted in white and red on the wall shown in this view. The kitchen is hidden behind the tower-like wood structure which dominates the entire area.

Below : Mr and Mrs Reginald Grady softened their San Francisco kitchen-dining room with painted flower motifs and a large chandelier. The table is covered with an apple-green cloth.

The London fashion designers and writers, Julian and Renée Robinson, converted the basement of their Georgian house into the huge kitchen-dining-living room shown here in four views. The impressive collection of early kitchen utensils distributed round the walls and on the dressers create a series of still-life pictures. A long refectory table, oil- and gas-lamps (which still work), an island counter, a pair of stoves, Provençal floor tiles and the comfortable leather sofas arranged one on either side of the old fireplace are some of the features that make one want to spend hours and hours in this room just looking.

TRADITIONAL
DINING ROOMS

This dining room designed by Anthony Denney for his country-house in Essex is very much a re-creation of a seventeenth-century English room. The panelling, the gate-legged table, the crystal chandelier, the portraits . . . all emulate the period. But the chairs, painted in the manner of the portrait frame, represent a decisively modern departure.

Opposite page : The dining room in Mrs Ferdinand Smith's San Francisco house combines traditional furniture in an interesting way. The dark table and sideboard and the white and gilt lacquered chairs are unified by the strong colour of the carpet and walls and also by the imposing crystal chandelier. The handsome eighteenth-century painting, which balances the window area, adds to the grandeur.

Except for the fact that the earliest dining rooms were short on chairs (normally everyone in Europe used to sit on benches, except for the head of the family who was the chairman) the traditional dining room has hardly changed in four hundred years. Cupboards, clocks, side-tables and various embellishments have been moved in and out according to tastes and prosperity. Walls have been hung with fabric; they have been panelled, painted, and covered with wallpaper. Paintings, including family portraits, and sculptures have also decorated the dining room at one stage or another. And today the traditional dining room is always imitative, at least in feeling if not in the actual use of antique furniture.

Opposite: A Mexican dining room in the early California hou belonging to costume designer Edith Head. It is true in ever detail with its brick and carved wood, its earthy colouring, an its pots, solid chairs and settle. Chequered mirrors repeat th pierced wall next to them, and a series of pierced iron shelv support a collection of Mexican glass.

A long refectory table is covered with damask in this cool, vaulted store room in the Villa dei Vescovi, near Padua. The carved wood figure at the end of the room, the early candlesticks, the lamps and side-table make this room look much the way any room of its size and type would have looked centuries ago. The small difference lies in the brilliant colours of the goblets' plates and table linen.

Right: The dining room in the author's sixteenth-century English farmhouse retains the mood of the old hall eating area with brick floors, elm refectory table and country elm chairs. In earlier days benches would have been used, rather than chairs. The walls which used to exist on either side of the fireplace have been cut away to give more space and light. Other modern touches are the printed cotton tablecloth which matches the border on the heavy woven cotton blinds, and the white-painted beams.

Opposite: Before the days of porcelain, it was usual to decorate tables at banquets with small sugar figures. The Meissen factory was quick to take advantage of the custom and to translate it into porcelain. The result was a whole series of eighteenth-century tables covered with charming, rather fey figures which were nicely calculated to keep the conversation going. This English dining room, belonging to Mr Harry Lebus, is well within the eighteenth-century tradition. The table setting is exquisite with its pagoda centre-piece, porcelain figures, gold, silver, mother-of-pearl and ormolu.

Indigo-blue paint picked out in white was used in this dining room in the eighteenth-century house belonging to Norman St John Stevas, M.P. in London. With his passion for Victoriana, Mr St John Stevas has up-dated the period, using nineteenth-century furniture, brass curtain poles, a crystal drop chandelier and portraits of Albert, the Prince Consort, and his tender young wife, Queen Victoria. The archway and counter-top on the left of the room conceal the kitchen with its elegant collection of blue and white china. But the room has a lightness and vivacity which, alas, the Victorians hardly ever achieved.

Right: Paul Anstee built this dining room into a nineteenth-century London house for Dr and Mrs Sportoletti Baduel. By the judicious use of pillars in carved and waxed pine he divided off one section of the very large room to make an ante-room, or tiny casual sitting room, where drinks are served before and after dinner. In the main room the ivory walls, pale ginger carpet, and the blue and grey Oriental rug provide a suitable background colour for the blue-fringed tablecloth and chairs. Curtains are in the same blue, edged with a delicately curved and shirred braid. The double row of prints are early Italian.

This dining room belonging to John Sinai, in San Francisco, was designed by Anthony Haile, using one of Mr Sinai's own fabric designs for the wall covering and curtaining. The table and chairs (with red-leather seats) are solidly traditional late eighteenth century.

The traditional dining room well translated into late twentieth-century American terms. The candelabra is here, but supplemented by inset spots in the ceiling. The polished wood table is also here but it has a twin. Both tables are encircled by comfortable upholstered armchairs standing on deep, lushly piled oatmeal carpeting. A large Chinese painting on one of the beige walls is set off by a mirror on one side and by two Chinese vases on the other. Val Arnold decorated the house for Mr and Mrs Daniel Schwartz of Palm Springs, California.

Opposite: Marbled paper walls in black and white with a double white border at the cornice and skirting, black shiny Edwardian chairs, an intricately designed white-painted table base and screen and a unique picture of dogs on the wall are the principal ingredients in a room that in spite of them all manages to look rural. The detail of the window-sill with white curtain fabric matching the squabs on the chairs, is filled with flowers in differing containers charmingly juxtaposed against a flower painting. The room is in the Westchester house belonging to and designed by Edward Zajac.

Above and right: A traditional room filled with spectacular silver belonging to Mr and Mrs Jules Stein in Los Angeles. Two extremely rare Sheffield plate-warmers stand on either side of the bay with its long curtains, festoon blinds and table stacked with silver *objets*. A mural is painted on the walls, and the glossy floor is topped with a luxurious Chinese rug.

This dining room designed by Mr John Wisner is a part of his totally Japanese house. All of it is beautifully detailed: the low red-lacquered tables, the embroidered cushions on the matting floor, the pearly light from the window-screens, the natural woods, the exquisite porcelain, and the large delicately painted screen.

The refectory table, leather chairs, dresser, candelabra, shaggy rug and brilliant crimson walls make this dining room an essentially American re-creation. Michael Taylor designed it for Mr and Mrs Roberts in San Francisco.

Opposite: Fleur Cowles's dining room in her sixteenth-century English country farmhouse has warm brick floors, white walls and exposed beams. The room provides a beautiful background for her proverbial entertaining and is a showplace for her collections of Provençal tablecloths, china, a long tableful of dummy fruit, vegetables and food – and also, of course, for her paintings.

MODERN
DINING
ROOMS

The modern dining room – or at least the dining room that breaks away completely from tradition – is rare. Occasionally one sees a room that makes use of such totally different materials that it seems to set a new environmental concept for eating. More usually, the modern dining room is a juxtaposition of old forms with non-traditional colouring; a new treatment of the walls and furniture, or a total use of the best of modern furnishings that owe nothing in shape or material to the past. Sometimes it is just a lightness of touch and colour, a clarity of view. In any event, the modern dining room makes a conscious attempt to break from tradition or else to use that tradition as a springboard for further ideas.

Sapphire-blue burlap on the walls and ceiling of this unusual dining room form a protective casing for the Saarinen chairs, the round table with its printed cotton cloth, and the modern chandelier which suggests a giant transparent sea-urchin. The console table is half of a large gilt table; the other half is used at the other side of the room. The setting was designed by William McCarty for Dr Al Kaplan.

Opposite: The classic modern dining table and chairs designed by Eero Saarinen appear in York Castle, the splendid Moroccan house which Yves Vidal and Charles Sevigny restored. The pure white against the arched grilled Moorish windows, the Baroque lantern and Moorish copper utensils on the white side-tables prove how classics of the twentieth century transcend time and location.

Right: The dining room in Ken and Kathleen Tynan's house was problematical as heating ducts ran under the ceiling and spoiled an otherwise quite beautiful nineteenth-century room. William McCarty solved the problem by painting the ceiling and its network of ducts a dense black and by suspending white-painted geometric slats of wood interlaced with low-voltage spots just below it. He painted the walls a lacquer red and panelled them with thin strips of glossy black wood. The floor was painted black, and the coconut-matting was sprayed white. A piece of white-painted branch decorates the fireplace, a Bridget Riley hangs above, and the pink and red covered table is surrounded by black polypropylene chairs.

Left: Mrs Mark Littman's London dining room with its antler candelabra, its cool green chairs and serving-tables, its palms and grassy table-cloth against the hot tones of the wall fabric, is a little like the owner herself: witty, nearly conforming, then rearing with graceful originality out of the way.

Opposite: Val Arnold is a young Californian designer with a nostalgic touch that has a sting in its tail. His dining room is covered with a paisley design in red and green on a yellow background. The carpet and chair seats are the moss-green of the walls and a large bunch of dried flowers at the far end of the room picks up all the colours he has used in the room. A weighty abstract composition on the right wall makes much of his own initial.

Opposite: Max Clendinning could well be Britain's most original designer. This dining room in his Georgian house is an extension of Art Deco, not a copy, or even a spoof. Walls are a gunmetal grey overpainted with a curvaceous pattern of pale grey, white, chrome-yellow, mauve-pink, white and scarlet. The window is left uncurtained, and the glass and wood table, the cut-out chairs and the grey-painted cupboard to the left of the fireplace are all early prototypes of his furniture. The chair in the foreground, upholstered in red, is a later prototype. The painted pattern on the wall was the result of one week-end's work.

Right: Allessandro d'Albrizzi designed this plexiglass and glass dining room for Miss Vivian Clore. Mirrored walls and ceiling reflect the blue and white Albrizzi carpet, bounce mysterious lights from the octagon of blue plexiglass cut into the ceiling and exaggerate, endlessly, the glass and plexiglass table. Downlights are set into the ceiling glass to cast pools on the floor.

Architect Arthur Elrod's dining room is tucked under the great spokes of concrete that fan out to support the roof of his house. The splayed metal chair legs, the slim disc of rosewood on the table-top which matches the rosewood wall, the great blue, grey and white abstract painting, the tropical plants and the polished stone floor all keep it very much in the twentieth-century idiom.

Opposite: This beautiful room belongs to Mr and Mrs Leslie Land in a house converted from an old barn. The brilliant red table against the terracotta of the boldly criss-crossed tiled floor, the blue and white of chair upholstery and ceramics, the green marbled frame of the long mirror and the ruched white of the festoon blinds against the delicate tracery of the candelabra synthesize into a harmonious whole.

DUAL-PURPOSE DINING ROOMS

Space is so rare a currency in most cities that the dining room proper, if it has not already been usurped by the kitchen, is more normally part of the main living room, or at least shares a dual function with the hall or library and, occasionally, with a bedroom of the studio-couch variety. Even if there is a formal dining room, it is often convenient to have a table in the sitting room for the enjoyment of more casual meals. The problem is to infiltrate and integrate the dining apparatus so subtly that it is hardly noticeable when the room is used for sitting, and yet dominates and attracts when the table is to be used for dining.

Above : The art dealer, David Edge, has made a spectacular house out of the harem of the former Sultan's Palace in Tangier. Banana trees and palms grow in the central arched space on to which open the main living area and the bedroom. There are no outside windows and the only external views are from the garden terraces above. The dining-sitting area shown here, with its enormous silver candelabras surrounded by foliage, its deep armchairs, Oriental rugs and Chinese antiquities, is comfortably flamboyant.

Opposite : Mr and Mrs Philip Stern's house in Washington, designed by the architect Hugh Newell Jacobsen, is a blaze of colour and painting interspersed with comfort and sculpture. The dining room is a splendid cool museum with its yellow and blue-jade walls, its long metal and glass table, its embossed ceiling embedded with spotlights, and its series of paintings and sculpture.

Opposite: A wide hall used as a dining room. The walls are a moss-green, outlined with white woodwork. The ceiling is white and so are the Saarinen table and chairs, the latter set with brown tweed cushions. Spots on the ceiling light up the sketches by the owner's architect husband, the late Ray Wilson. The upright piano with its bowlful of daisies is painted white.

The dining-sitting room is a common state of affairs in small modern houses all over the world. The one shown above, designed by the author, and using Max Clendinning's furniture, was in an exhibition house for Wren Properties. Walls, furniture, lilies and fur rugs are off-white, the carpet is oatmeal and the only touches of colour are the single red-lacquered frame of one chair and the green leaves of the palms.

This sitting room-dining room in Jack Lenor Larsen's New York apartment is full of lovely detail: chain-mail curtains, a pair of Victorian cane chaises-longues arranged on either side of the plexiglass and glass table, and the striped red fabric for window wall and blinds which contrast with the electric blue of the paint.

Opposite: This dining area in Tony Duquette's Hollywood studio is surrounded, quite deliberately, by every decorational fob, including a huge tapestry, elongated screens, a portrait on an easel, a mass of strong-scented lilies, a couch massed with tiger-skin, leopard-skin and silk cushions, a tablecloth which looks like snake-skin, and chairs covered with leopard.

The top floor of Christina Smith's Covent Garden warehouse was turned by Max Clendinning into a general open-plan living area incorporating bathroom, kitchen, sitting and dining area. Three views of it are shown here. The entire space, painted red and white, is divided by a series of low and tall units and cupboards and shelves, which act variously as dressing-tables, desks, serving-tables, sofa backs, seat bases and what you will. The steeply pitched rafters are all white except for a square frame near the top which is scarlet. The long wood table on its metal base is partnered by white bentwood chairs.

When space is a problem, a combination dining area and library is an eminently sensible solution, as demonstrated by designer William McCarty in Mr and Mrs Cob Stenham's house. Bookshelves climb up to the high ceiling with its elaborate Victorian cornice. The khaki-brown and parchment coloured wallpaper was designed by Osborne and Little, and the carpet picks up the dominant tone of the paper.

The first-floor area of this Boston house, converted by Tom Green, consists of a kitchen (behind the brilliant chrome-yellow and scarlet support to the balcony), a dining area with scarlet and white Marimekko cloth, and a conversation area with red Magistretti chairs, a glass table and orange rug. All these brilliant colours are constrained and framed by the bare brick walls and the wall of the balcony.

Right : A comfortable complex of dining, living and kitchen areas was worked out by Peter Panakker. This view shows a round, gate-legged table with oak chairs placed just outside the carved wood kitchen units.

Below : A splendid spiral staircase of steel twists up from floor to floor in Mr and Mrs David Harrison's house. The dining room, with its tiled floor, Oriental rug and biscuit-coloured walls, is a good foil for the South American paintings and plexiglass sculpture. Even the staircase seems a piece of sculpture in its own right.

ACKNOWLEDGMENTS

I was greatly helped in preparing this book by Ishbel Ross's *Taste in America* and Doreen Yarwood's *The English Home*. Naturally, as in any book of this sort, nothing could have been produced at all but for the patience of all those hungry and frustrated people who could not get into their kitchens and dining rooms while my photographers were working. It says a great deal for their fortitude, that not only were they pleasant and agreeable about the whole thing, but in many cases they fed us most deliciously as well.

I am particularly indebted to my many friends in America, in particular Mrs Sarah Tomerlin Lee, Mrs Barbara Plumb, Mrs Alison Harwood, Miss Mary Jane Poole, Mrs Jeanne Weekes Oppenheimer, Dr and Mrs Alexander Preston, Mr and Mrs Roger Spalding, Miss Ruth Hornsey, Mr and Mrs Lester Cole and Mrs Barbara Poe for their enormous assistance and help; to Mr John Ambrose for lending me his patient support; to Michael Boys, for allowing me to use a photograph; and to my family for not minding me keeping out of the kitchen once in a while.

M.G.

The decorative illustrations on the front pages of the book are: Copper pans on dresser in the Brighton Pavilion (frontispiece); Sixteenth-century English knife, Courtesy The Victoria and Albert Museum (title-page); Pennsylvania Dutch painted tray, Courtesy Landis Valley Museum (copyright page); Roman spoon, Courtesy The British Museum (contents page).